# Eric's
## Thai
## Travel Diary

by

### Eric

With help from
Louise Schofield (story) and
Rae Dale (illustrations)

## KEEP OUT!
(That means you)

# NELSON
## CENGAGE Learning™

**Eric's Thai Travel Diary**

Text: Louise Schofield
Illustrations: Rae Dale
Editor: Kate Daniel
Design: Leigh Ashforth
Reprint: Siew Han Ong

**PM Extras Chapter Books**
**Sapphire Level 29 Set A**
The Bommyknocker Tree
The Man Who Measured the World
Eric's Thai Travel Diary
H for Horrible
'Jungle Trek
Lizard Tongue

Text © 2004 Louise Schofield
Illustrations © 2004 Cengage Learning Australia Pty Limited

ISBN 978 0 17 011713 5
ISBN 978 0 17 011709 8 (set)

**Cengage Learning Australia**
Level 7, 80 Dorcas Street
South Melbourne, Victoria Australia 3205
Phone: 1300 790 853

**Cengage Learning New Zealand**
Unit 4B Rosedale Office Park
331 Rosedale Road, Albany, North Shore NZ 0632
Phone: 0508 635 766

For learning solutions, visit **cengage.com.au**

Printed in China by 1010 Printing International Ltd
12 15

# Contents

# CHAPTER 1

# The
# Diary Bug

Dear Mrs Smith and Class-buddies,

After keeping diaries of my trips to Nepal and Greece, I can't help myself. I've caught the dreaded diary bug again. I have no choice but to write about my trip to yet another exotic country – Thailand this time.

As you know, my parents love to travel, although they don't travel with each other anymore – only me (that's one of the downsides of divorce, I guess; if only they would understand that I'd rather be with my best friend, Pete).

But when Dad called from Bangkok and asked if I wanted to spend part of the holidays with him, how could I refuse? He's been working there for three months and he's missed me.

See ya later, Alligator!

YIPPPPEEEE!! – Eric

# CHAPTER 2

# On My Way!

So here I am on the plane – ALL BY MYSELF. Pete was soooooo impressed that I was travelling alone that he came to the airport with Mum to see me off.

Mum got all teary and embarrassing. I told her not to worry, that Dad will be there to pick me up. I promised to send her a postcard and Pete an email.

I've just found Bangkok on the map. It's the capital. Now... what channel is the movie on?

You have to remember that my Dad is a very busy man. When he's home, he has secretaries who arrange stuff for him. So, don't be surprised to learn that HE WASN'T AT THE AIRPORT TO MEET ME!!

After I got over a mild attack of panic (okay, a MAJOR attack), I found the place to collect my bag. Airports are the same everywhere I reckon.

I didn't have Dad's phone number (that was dumb), but I had the address of his hotel. And I had some Thai money. Thai money is called baht – pronounced Bart, as in Bart Simpson.

The guys at the taxi rank outside looked surprised to see a kid on his own. However, once they saw I could pay for my fare, they opened the door and I got in. The ride through Bangkok was crazy, but soon I was in the foyer of Dad's hotel. They called Dad's room.

Dad got down there pretty quick. He looked shocked. He thought the plane wasn't due until tomorrow.

Like I said, Dad is a busy man, but he's cool. He made up for it by taking me out to a special dinner. My mouth has been burning ever since. Gosh, it had a lot of chilli in it! And we talked about football and school for ages.

After dinner, there was some special Thai dancing. The dancers were all dressed up in fancy Thai clothes, and the lady dancers amazed me with how they moved their hands.

Some pretty cool guys played music on traditional instruments.

9

# CHAPTER 3

# City of Angels

Dad says Bangkok is called the City of Angels. The angels are pretty noisy though – the traffic is wild!

After breakfast, Dad took me exploring. Not far from our hotel is a jetty where you can catch a boat to take you up or down the river, the Chao Phrya (Chow Prii-ya). Dad says he catches boats as often as possible because they're usually faster and it's more relaxing than travelling in the busy streets.

We lined up; then when a boat pulled over for a second or two, we jumped on.

First we got off at Bangkok's Grand Palace. It's top of the tourist list and for good reason.

It sparkles! It shines! It's sensational! But we didn't see any royalty. Perhaps they were busy.

Dad took a photo of me looking cool outside one of the royal buildings, pretending to be a prince. I wore the sunglasses I bought at a stall outside our hotel this morning. They were a bargain. I bought a pair for Pete too.

Next to the palace is The Temple of the Emerald Buddha, Wat Phra Kaew (Wot Pra Cow). Wat means temple.

Most Thai people are Buddhists, and Dad says this Buddha statue is one of the most important. We took off our shoes like everyone else and had a look inside. I could smell incense burning.

Most people sat or knelt on the floor praying. We sat too and rested; it was very peaceful. Dad says you must NEVER let the soles of your feet point at other people — and especially not the Buddha. It's rude in Thailand.

For lunch, we stopped for a bowl of phat thai (pah-t tie) – that's Thai for fried rice noodles. While we ate, Dad told me a bit about Buddhism.

It began a long time ago in India when a prince named Siddhartha left his palace, his family and all his money to learn the secret of happiness and peace.

He even left his beautiful wife and baby son, who he loved very much.

This prince guy wandered around with nothing and lived on what people gave him along the way. He also sat around and meditated a lot.

He knew that people were unhappy when they didn't have what they wanted, but he also noticed that money didn't make you happy either. He decided that if you learned how to stop wanting ANYTHING, you would find perfect happiness.

Perfect happiness is called Nirvana (Ner-varn-uh), and when the prince reached it he became The Buddha.

Sometimes you see Buddhist monks wandering the streets in Bangkok. They shave their hair off, wear yellow robes and carry a bowl around, just like The Buddha did.

It's difficult to understand how you can stop wanting everything, though. I want to breathe, I want to eat, I want to see Pete – surely they aren't much? But it made me think...

Dad and I went shopping in the afternoon. He bought me some t-shirts (I didn't want them, I just accepted them – just like Buddha) and then we went to a silk shop. Dad helped me buy a beautiful silk shirt for Mum.

When we got back to our hotel, we cooled off in the pool. Then Dad taught me some Thai words. Boy, the Thai language is sooooo different to English. The same word can mean something completely different if your voice goes up – or down. I was making some pretty funny sounds trying to get it right.

However, I can now say hello really well – sawat dii (souw-uh-dee).

# CHAPTER 4

# Shopping Afloat

Dad dragged me out of bed very early this morning to the floating markets of Bangkok. FLOATING markets?

We caught a boat with other people, and soon I found out how it gets its name. We came to a place where there were lots of people in small wooden boats selling fresh fruit, vegetables and flowers.

Dad bought some mangoes and bananas, after bargaining to get a good price. Then I bought us some fresh corn that had been cooked over coals. We took lots of photos.

Back on land, we wandered off for noodles at one of the street stalls – I was starving!

Afterwards, we visited the National Museum, then on the other side of the river we took a look at the royal barges inside a big shed.

These barges are amazing boats used during festivals; they are decorated with real gold! One of the barges is used by the king. I sent a postcard of this to Mum.

After a nap and a swim at the hotel we went out again. A taxi dropped us near a noisy street with flashing coloured lights and people everywhere.

Bangkok seems to be busier at night. I guess that's because it is cooler then, and lots of people go out to eat at the food stalls on the street and in the markets. I tried a special Thai soup made with coconut milk and chicken. There was stuff called lemon grass in it, and weird-shaped lime leaves.

# CHAPTER 5

# Indiana Eric & the Temples of Siam

Dad woke me up really early AGAIN and took me out for another exhausting day (and I thought this was a holiday!). But it was great!

First we caught a bus. It took about an hour and a half to get to this amazing place called Ayuthaya (Ay-yoo-tay-ya). It looks like something out of a movie, with lots of huge stone statues and temples all over the place.

According to my guidebook, Thailand used to be called Siam. Ayuthaya was the capital of Siam from 1350 to 1767.

You know, just when you think you've seen enough temples, you go to a place like this and change your mind. As I walked around, I imagined filming a movie here – starring me and Pete, of course!

Dad and I took heaps of photos. Some of the temples were in ruins, but others were restored and looked amazing. Actually, I thought they looked amazing even when they were in ruins!

We spent most of the day in Ayuthaya, then we caught the bus back to sticky Bangkok.

# CHAPTER 6

# My Island in the Sun

This morning, Dad and I caught a plane to an island in the south of Thailand called Koh Samui (Koh Sam-oo-ee). Koh means island. I don't know what Samui means.

We're staying in a bungalow with a hammock on the front porch and a great view of the beach. We swam and slept in the afternoon. Our holiday has really begun!

I met a boy who lives here. His name is Nu (Noo). His parents run one of the restaurants on our beach and we ate there tonight.

Nu's restaurant was great! Dad and I ordered a whole fried fish in a hot and sour sauce with rice. We watched Nu's mum first fry the fish in a wok until it was crispy. Then she fried up all kinds of spices, sauces and other stuff like palm sugar and poured the yummy mix over the fish. We ate it with hot rice.

Dad and I reckon it's the best meal we've ever had!

For dessert, we ate fruit salad with papaya, pineapple, fresh coconut and really sweet bananas with big, black pips in them. Dad said these were real bananas, the way they've been for hundreds of years – not like the bananas we buy in the shops back home. Ours have been bred to travel in trucks and sit on shop shelves.

After dinner we walked home along the beach. We could see the lights of boats, fishing for prawns and squid.

# Killer Coconuts!

What more do you want to do on a tropical island other than swim, lie in the sun, sleep and eat?

Well, I've always wanted to drink straight out of a freshly picked coconut with a straw, just like they do in the movies.

And that's what I did today...

Nu asked one of his friends to pick a fresh coconut from a palm near our bungalow. His friend had a pet monkey, trained to fetch coconuts – so up the tree the little fella went!

The monkey went straight to a coconut, then twisted it and twisted it until it fell down. THUMP!

The green coconuts are best for drinking. Nu's friend hacked off some of the stuff on the outside with a big knife, then nicked a hole for the straw. The taste was kind-of refreshing! Dad had one too.

Did you know that every year hundreds of people are killed by falling coconuts? When you hear them thump to the ground you understand why! KER-SPLAT!

So I've learnt that you must NEVER, EVER sunbake under a coconut tree. And when you walk through the jungle always follow the pathways that twist and wiggle around. These have been made by the local people, who know to avoid those killer coconuts!

Dad says you should always listen to what local people tell you, anywhere you visit. If you do, you'll have more fun – and you'll live longer too.

27

This afternoon, Nu found us some snorkelling gear and we went out together while Dad did some bodysurfing.

Nu showed me some reefs not far from our beach. We saw lots of fish and even a giant clam!

When we returned, some fishermen had pulled their boat onto the beach. They showed us what they'd caught, and carried all sorts of fish and crabs up to the restaurant.

# CHAPTER 8

# Last Day on Samui

Today's our last day on the island, so we decided to visit Koh Samui's port town, Na Thawn (Na Torn).

After breakfast, we caught one of the island taxi-buses. They're called songthaews (song-taows). Passengers climb in at the back and sit on benches.

There are no bus stops here. Songthaews stop just about anywhere along the main road. If you see one, you just wave for it to pick you up. They're great! The drivers toot their horns a lot.

In the town, Dad and I wandered along the waterfront looking at the ferries and fishing boats. We bought some sarongs – for us as well as Mum. Men wear sarongs too, and they are great for the beach. The batik sarongs come from Indonesia.

To make a batik, a pattern is drawn on fabric with hot wax. When the wax dries, the fabric is dyed one colour, then another pattern in hot wax is applied – and so on, until the fabric has several layers of coloured patterns. Oh, they take the dried wax off.

While Dad read the paper, I sent an email to Pete from an Internet cafe.

Sawat dii, Pete!

Dad and I have been kidnapped by bandits and dumped on a remote island in southern Thailand. It's called Koh Samui.

Fortunately, the natives are friendly. But there's nothing to do but swim, lie in hammocks and eat. It's tough! Would be a great location for a movie about two boys who survive a shipwreck.

If you jump on a plane and get here soon, you can meet my Thai friend Nu. We've been exploring all around our beach. Maybe he'd like to be in our movie too.

I'll be home to annoy you in a couple of days.

Eric ;-)

# CHAPTER 9

# Homeward Bound

My Thai holiday is almost over. Dad and I are on the plane flying back to Bangkok. We've had a great time – the best holiday we've had together!

Dad is staying in Bangkok, but I'm flying home tonight. I can't wait to give Pete his new sunglasses and tell him all my movie ideas.

I hope Mum remembers to pick me up from the airport. If she doesn't, Dad said to give her a hard time!